# WORSHIP IN MANY COLORS

*Creative Settings
of Hymns, Songs,
and Spirituals*

*Arranged for Solo Piano by*

# Melody Bober

**Lillenas** PUBLISHING COMPANY
KANSAS CITY, MO 64141

# CONTENTS

# O Worship the King

JOHANN MICHAEL HAYDN
*Arranged by Melody Bober*

With energy ♩ = ca. 116

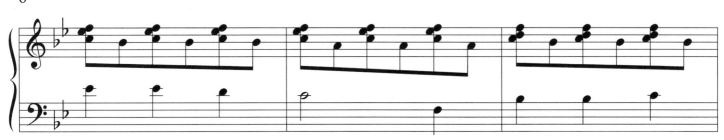

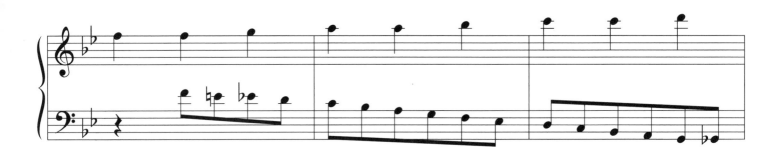

# Be Thou My Vision

Traditional Irish Melody
*Arranged by Melody Bober*

# My Faith Has Found a Resting Place

Norwegian Folk Melody
*Arranged by Melody Bober*

Lively ♩ = ca. 94

# 'Tis So Sweet to Trust in Jesus

WILLIAM J. KIRKPATRICK
*Arranged by Melody Bober*

**PLEASE NOTE: Copying of this product is not covered by CCLI licenses. For CCLI information call 1-800-234-2446.**

# Create in Me a Clean Heart

Unknown
*Arranged by Melody Bober*

Singing

decresc.

*mp*

mel.

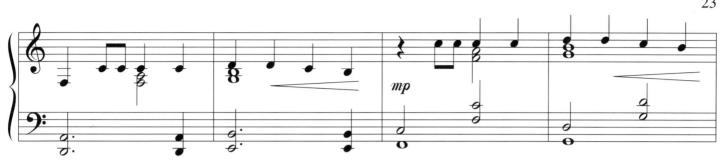

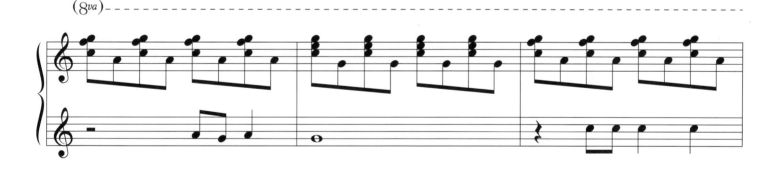

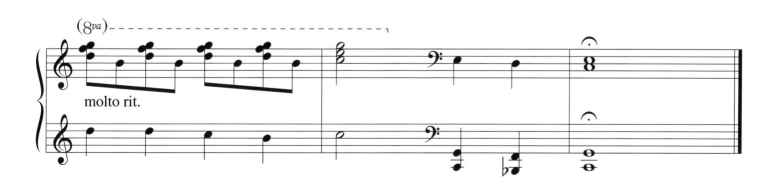

# I Am Thine, O Lord

WILLIAM H. DOANE
*Arranged by Melody Bober*

Flowing smoothly ♩ = ca. 112

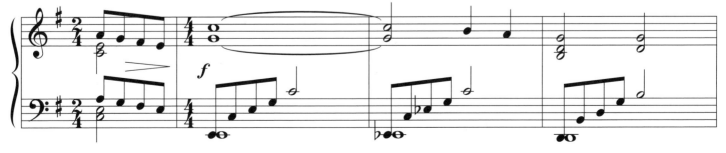

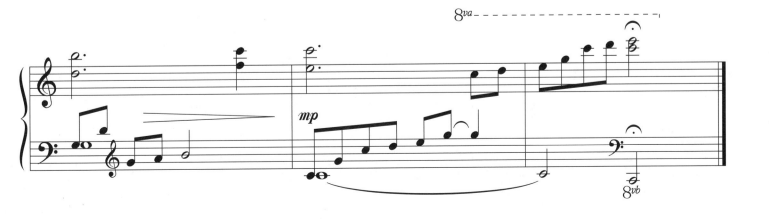

# I'm Gonna Let It Shine

### This Little Light of Mine
### Deep and Wide

Medium jazz swing ♩ = ca. 112

*Arranged by Melody Bober*

"This Little Light of Mine" (Traditional)

"Deep and Wide" (Traditional)

# Come, Join to Sing

Come, Christians, Join to Sing
This Is My Father's World
Blessed Assurance
Like a River Glorious

Joyful exuberance!  ♩ = ca. 120

*Arranged by Melody Bober*

"Come, Christians, Join to Sing" (Traditional)

*mf*

"This Is My Father's World" (Traditional)

"Blessed Assurance" (Phoebe Palmer Knapp)

"Like a River Glorious" (James Mountain)

# Jesus Is My Lord

Unknown
*Arranged by Melody Bober*

# Jesus Loves Me

WILLIAM B. BRADBURY
*Arranged by Melody Bober*

Reflective ♩ = ca. 92